We're Sailing to Galapagos
A Week in the Pacific

For my children: Bill, Margee, Beth and Ginger — L. K.

To Carlotta and Federico — G. R.

Barefoot Books
124 Walcot Street
Bath, BA1 5BG

This book has been printed on 100% acid-free paper

Graphic design by Judy Linard, London
Colour separation by Bright Arts, Singapore
Printed and bound in China by Printplus Ltd

This book was typeset in Clearface Bold
The illustrations were prepared with painted, cut papers combined with natural materials

Paperback ISBN 978-1-84686-101-7

British Cataloguing-in-Publication-Data:
a catalogue record for this book is available from the British Library

3 5 7 9 8 6 4

We're Sailing to Galapagos
A Week in the Pacific

written by Laurie Krebs

illustrated by Grazia Restelli

Barefoot Books
Celebrating Art and Story

Far out across the ocean,

Where the vast sky meets the sea,

Lie islands called Galapagos.

Come! Visit them with me.

We're sailing to Galapagos, Galapagos, Galapagos,
We're sailing to Galapagos.
I wonder who we'll see.

On Monday, giant tortoises,

With weathered shells of green,

Plod past us while they munch their lunch
Of vegetable cuisine.

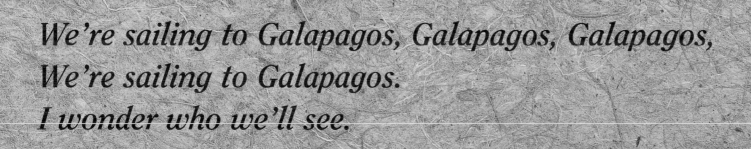

We're sailing to Galapagos, Galapagos, Galapagos,
We're sailing to Galapagos.
I wonder who we'll see.

On Tuesday, courting albatrosses,

Shaded grey and white,

Rehearse the drills of clacking bills

Until they get it right.

We're sailing to Galapagos, Galapagos, Galapagos,
We're sailing to Galapagos.
I wonder who we'll see.

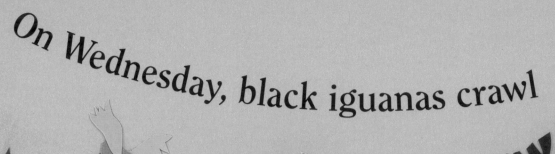

On Wednesday, black iguanas crawl

Together in a swarm.

They love to sleep piled in a heap.

It helps to keep them warm.

We're sailing to Galapagos, Galapagos, Galapagos,
We're sailing to Galapagos.
I wonder who we'll see.

On Thursday, skipping lava crabs,

With shells of brilliant red,

Find food that hides in ebbing tides

Across the lava bed.

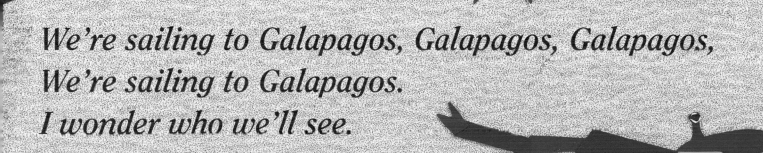

We're sailing to Galapagos, Galapagos, Galapagos,
We're sailing to Galapagos.
I wonder who we'll see.

On Friday, blue-foot boobies fish

Along the rocky shore.

They feed their chicks who nest on sticks,

Then they fly back for more.

We're sailing to Galapagos, Galapagos, Galapagos,
We're sailing to Galapagos.
I wonder who we'll see.

On Saturday, brown sea lions snooze

Outstretched upon the beach.

Then flippers flip! They take a dip

And swim beyond our reach.

We're sailing to Galapagos, Galapagos, Galapagos,
We're sailing to Galapagos.
I wonder who we'll see.

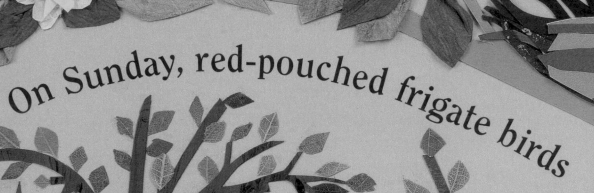

On Sunday, red-pouched frigate birds

Are not to be outdone.

To woo a mate, their chests inflate,

Impressing everyone.

We've visited Galapagos, Galapagos, Galapagos,
We've visited Galapagos
And this is who we've seen:

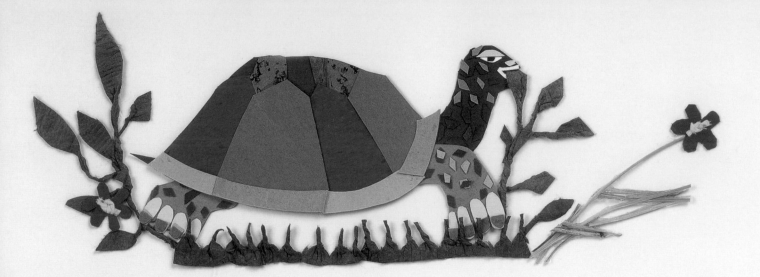

Plodding tortoises,

Clacking albatrosses,

Sleeping iguanas,

Skipping lava crabs,

Fishing booby birds,

Swimming sea lions,

and courting frigate birds.

Far out across the ocean,

Where the water meets the sky,

We've visited Galapagos

And now we wave 'Goodbye'.

The Galapagos Islands

The Galapagos Islands belong to the South American country of Ecuador. They are located in the Pacific Ocean, six hundred miles west of the mainland. Over millions of years, they have been formed, one by one, from underwater volcanoes that spew lava up from the bottom of the sea. Today, this chain of barren islands is home to a variety of plants, animals and birds that have gradually adapted to life there.

Because they were created at different times, each island is unique. Some of the older ones have steep slopes and misty weather. Some have fields of grass and dry weather. Many of the newer islands are covered with carpets of rocky, ropy lava which look like lanes of hardened chocolate. So, unlike most Pacific islands, there are no big palm trees or miles of beaches, only small bushes, desert plants and narrow strips of sand.

Set in the tropics where it is usually very hot, the Galapagos Islands are bathed in cool currents that flow in from the Antarctic. These streams mix with warm waters from the equator to control the islands' weather. The currents also bring a rich supply of food for the creatures who live there.

At first, the Galapagos Islands were nothing but beds of lava. It took hundreds of years before anything could live or grow there. Gradually, the barren rocks crumbled into soil and tiny plants grew from the seeds brought by wind, water and migrating birds. Scientists have found proof that tortoises floated out from South America on westward currents. They think other creatures swam or hitched rides on logs that carried them hundreds of miles. Birds, flying across the ocean, stopped to raise their families on the islands. Only the strongest of these creatures survived and reproduced. Now each island has its own unique collection of wildlife and plant life.

People have known about the Galapagos Islands for nearly five hundred years. The first visitors were pirates and whalers who landed to search for fresh water and tortoise meat. The most famous visitor to the islands was Charles Darwin, who came to study the plants and animals. Today, some people live on four of the islands, but most of the visitors are tourists who come to see 'The Islands of the Tortoises' and the remarkable creatures who make their home there.

The Creatures of Galapagos

This story features just a few of the creatures that live in the Galapagos Islands. Below, you can learn about them and read about others too.

Blue-Footed Boobies

Blue-footed boobies are noted for their comical behaviour as well as their remarkable blue feet. They are expert fishermen, dive-bombing from mid-air and hurtling into the water at incredible speeds. Both parents care for the young, bringing home the fish found close to shore.

Darwin's Finches

Sparrow-sized and drab, Darwin's finches are nevertheless very interesting to scientists who study them. The finches are believed to come from a common ancestor, yet over the years, they have developed specialised beaks and distinct eating habits depending on which island they inhabit.

Frigate Birds

To attract a mate flying overhead, male frigate birds puff up their red chest pouches to the size of a small football. Then, calling aloud, they turn their heads and wings upwards and shake themselves vigorously. Frigate birds are excellent fishermen, but are also well known for stealing food from others.

Fur Seals

Fur seals are a type of sea lion. Their thick, dense coats distinguish them from their larger 'cousins'. For many years, they were hunted for their prized skins. Now fur seals are protected by law and can be seen swimming in cool waters or resting in the shade of steep rocks along the rugged shore.

Galapagos Doves

With bright red feet and a brilliant blue ring around their eyes, Galapagos doves are splendid-looking birds. Their reddish-brown feathers are set off by pink tinges on their breasts and iridescent patches of bronze-green on their necks. Galapagos doves feed mostly on the seeds and pulp of cactus plants.

Galapagos Hawks

Galapagos hawks are fearless birds of prey with keen eyesight and few enemies among the islands' creatures. They hunt young birds, lizards, small iguanas, rats and insects. As scavengers, they feed on nearly any dead animal and serve as the Galapagos rubbish disposal unit.

Galapagos Mockingbirds

Tame, curious and unafraid of humans, Galapagos mockingbirds form a welcoming committee for visitors to the islands. They often act as large family groups who co-operate in raising a new brood of chicks, foraging for food and defending the borders of their territory.

Galapagos Penguins

Most penguins are found in the frigid waters of Antarctica but Galapagos penguins live in tropical waters, north of the equator. Unable to fly like other birds, and awkward when walking on land, they are masterful swimmers, using their wings to hurtle themselves forward and their feet to steer.

Galapagos Sea Lions

Colonies of sea lions soak up the sun along sandy beaches when they aren't fishing or romping with one another in the water. Sociable and curious, they are a great favourite among visitors to the islands who are sometimes lucky enough to snorkel or kayak alongside the playful pups.

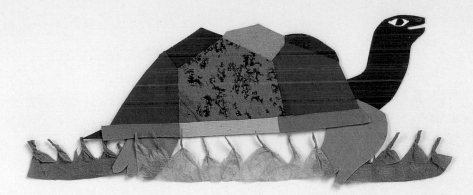

Giant Tortoises

As well as being the symbol of the Galapagos Islands, giant tortoises have two other claims to fame. They are the largest tortoises in the world, often weighing more than 180 kilograms, and they live for a very long time. Scientists think some of the tortoises are between 100 and 150 years old.

Land Iguanas

Wearing an impressive row of spines down their backs, yellowish-brown land iguanas are found in the driest part of the islands. They get liquid from their favourite food, prickly pear cactus pads. Their tough mouths are able to chew the spiky pads without even scraping away the sharp thorns.

Marine Iguanas

The only sea-going lizards in the world, marine iguanas feed on algae found along tide-lines. They are expert divers and can remain under water for up to an hour. They pile up on lava rocks to rest, keep warm and 'sneeze' out the ocean's salt which gives them a white hairdo.

Masked Boobies

Although masked boobies usually hatch two eggs, just one baby survives. The stronger chick attacks the weaker one, pushing it out of the nest to die of hunger or wide temperature changes. This may seem cruel, but on the barren islands, booby parents can find only enough food for one healthy chick.

Marine Turtles

For most of the year, marine turtles live under water and are rarely seen. However, at nesting time, females come ashore to dig large pits in the sand, using their back legs as shovels. Into the pits, they lay seventy or eighty eggs and bury them deep in the sand before returning to the sea.

Red-Billed Tropicbirds

With dark red bills and graceful white tail streamers, these spectacular birds are easily spotted against a backdrop of black lava cliffs, where they make their homes. Landing on their nests is difficult and the holes are so small that their elegant feathers droop over the ledge and give away their hiding places.

Red-Footed Boobies

The most amazing thing about red-footed boobies is their feet. Bright red! As they nest in bushes or small trees rather than on the ground like other boobies, their colourful feet are often hidden from view. But sharp eyes may see the red reflected from their feet on to their feathered breasts.

Red Lava Crabs

Red lava crabs are also called Sally Lightfoot crabs because of the way they skip across puddles on the lava rocks. They often keep company with marine iguanas, following the tides in and out, day and night, eating bits of algae. When disturbed, they squirt out water like a water pistol.

Waved Albatrosses

Waved albatross partners stand face to face to perform their long, noisy courting display. With yellow bills clacking, they bow their heads and arch their necks, rehearsing a precise routine over and over. Once the ritual is perfected, the birds mate for life and, together, care for their young.

It remains a mystery how land birds ever reached the Galapagos Islands. Unlike seabirds, they aren't equipped to fly long distances and scientists believe they were first swept to the islands by the fierce winds of storms.

Charles Darwin

Charles Darwin was only twenty years old when he left England to join the crew of the HMS Beagle. He always loved science and, as a boy, had spent many hours studying and collecting plants, insects and rocks. In 1831, he was invited to join the Beagle's expedition as a naturalist. It was rare in those days to have someone aboard the ship who could read and write as well as gather scientific data. Charles Darwin was the perfect man for the job.

One of the places Darwin visited during his five-year voyage was the Galapagos Islands. Here, he recorded information about many plants, animals and birds. As he worked, he wondered how the creatures had reached the islands in the first place, and how they survived on the barren volcanic rock. He also wondered why the same animal looked a little different from one island to the next.

When Darwin returned to England, he studied his notes, pondered what he had seen, and studied some more. Several years later, in 1859, he wrote a book called *The Origin of Species.* The book described a whole new way of looking at how living things change, or evolve, over many years. What Charles Darwin learned on his trip to Galapagos led to new scientific theories to consider. Today, his ideas remain as one of the ways some people think about the natural world.